Poetry   £5

DONALD SMITH is Director of the Sco
Edinburgh's Netherbow and a founder of t
From 1982 to 2003 he was responsible
Netherbow Theatre, producing, directing,
sional theatre and community dramas, as
and storytelling events. The current rebuilding of the Netherbow pro-
vided a rare opportunity to gather some of his own creative work, which
ebbs and flows between poetry and performance.

By the same author:

Memory Hill (Diehard Drama, 2002)
Storytelling Scotland: A Nation in Narrative (Polygon, 2001)
History of Scottish Theatre (co-author, Mainstream, 1998)
Celtic Travellers (Stationery Office, 1997)
Celtic Journeys (SCCC, 1997)
John Knox House: Gateway to the Old Town (John Donald
     Publishers Ltd, 1996)
Edinburgh Old Town Pilgrims' Way (John Pearson, 1995)
The Scottish Stage (Candlemaker Press, 1994)

A Long Stride
Shortens the Road

POEMS OF SCOTLAND
by
DONALD SMITH

Luath Press Limited

EDINBURGH

www.luath.co.uk

First Published 2004

The paper used in this book is recyclable. It is made from low
chlorine pulps produced in a low energy, low emission manner from
renewable forests.

The publisher acknowledges subsidy from

 Scottish **Arts** Council

towards the publication of this volume.

Printed and bound by
DigiSource (GB) Ltd., Livingston

Typeset in 10.5 Sabon by S. Fairgrieve 0131 658 1763

For Mairi, Duncan, Kirstin,
Andrew and Neil

Contents

A Long Stride Shortens the Road
Poems 1979 – 2004

THE POEMS IN THIS collection belong to a period in which Scotland's political identity was called into question by the failed referendum of 1979, distorted by eighteen years of imposed right-wing government, and then accorded a devolved form of home rule in 1997. Being Scotland, the reconvening of a Scottish Parliament in 1999 was followed by a period of self-questioning and dissonance. These events imbued every aspect of my development as I struggled to achieve an intellectual and creative pathway consonant with what had formed my own sense of personal, social and spiritual identity. The restoration of Scotland's political identity has been, for me, an artistic liberation.

These issues, which affected so many people in Scotland, were complicated in my own case by individual factors. Having been born David Coulter of Irish parentage, I spent the first few months of my life in an orphanage in Glasgow. I was then adopted into a Church of Scotland manse and christened Donald Smith.

By instinct, rather than information, I was never satisfied with my situation. While acknowledging the huge benefits I gained from adoption and the generous support of my adoptive parents, I could not accept that these circumstances were better than my 'natural state', which was of course an offshoot of 'sin'. For many years I remained ignorant of my own origins.

Consequently I had to shape my cultural and spiritual reference points from what Scotland gave me. The poems display inadequately how rich that context and inheritance is, even to an Irish exile. There are poems of gratitude, love songs for a country in which so many Scots are afraid to have faith, as well as dramatic voices echoing the conflicts and arguments that engender change. Many of these poems were originally published in literary magazines. I thank Tessa Ransford of *Lines Review*, Raymond Ross of *Cencrastus*, Joy Hendry of *Chapman* magazine, and Stewart Conn the Edinburgh City Makar for their support and encouragement. Robin Thomson made *Cradle King* a dramatic enactment.

Scotland is more able these days to speak its own name with its own voices, though we are still wrestling with what such namings might mean, both for our social present and our political future. The opening of the new Scottish Parliament, an undoubted artistic masterpiece is a moment for affirmation, an appropriation of buried continuities, or at the very least an interval of hope.

Donald Smith
Edinburgh 2004

Man and Boy

Man and Boy
for Hamish Henderson

One

One May morning, a little boy,
I crept out early to the glistening dew.
But as I climbed the glen
Mist wrapped itself around me
Like a tattered standard, and the high hills
Peeked over cloaks of cloud.
The burn dodged and twisted, clambering
Till lost into a borderland of marshy tussock.
Near the source I ran aground
And stopped to watch the valley clear.
Looming through the mist
A giant figure stretched his early morning
Shadow to my side. A rollicky tilt,
Hands flailed then sank into the pockets
Of a wrunkled cardigan, matching hat on head,
A collie dog at heel and steel eyes
Glittering behind lopsided spectacles.
'How are you laddie?' 'All right.'
Strands of loose white hair spreadeagled
In the breeze on ruddy cheeks.
'What are you doing up here?' 'Thinkin.'
'Aye, just so. On a May morning.'
We listened in his silence
To the music of the curlew and the plover
As the mist dispersed before a laverock air.
'Gaelic' he said, 'they sing in Gaelic,

The language behind the speech.'
Then abruptly he was off with louping stride
And I scuttled after to keep up.
'Time for travelling' he intoned.
'We've dragged our feet for far too long.'

Two

Level at the rucksack eyes
Rise and falling with his breath
White haired, bonneted and cropped

A long stride shortens the road

Off the path, splash through the stream
Because this was Adomnan's ford
Columba's light in a leather satchel

A long stride shortens the road

Down amongst the littered rocks
Finn's band hunted, Diarmid stretched
His length against the prickly boar

A long stride shortens the road

Rest a moment at the hillside cairn
The Gregarach proscribed and torched
Rob Roy battleless from Sherrifmuir

A long stride shortens the road

Tumbledown of wet grass, boulders
Mark the deserted townships clearing
Crofters to the margin, emigrants world wide

A long stride shortens the road

The burgh's sentryless by day
Boots clashing on the stony setts
Together cross the Lowland bridge

A long stride shortens the road

Shoulder to shoulder past the Tolbooth court
Tree hung for liberty, life
Raps for death at the castle gate

A long stride shortens the road

Fields of battle are spread below
Scots with Bruce and Wallace bled
Can sing Mandela's anthem now

A long stride shortens the road

Three

The single decker crawled interminably
Through linear villages that broke their banks
With regimented houses and breeze blocks
Spilling shapelessly across the land.
Grey country on a lowering afternoon
Lit by brazen signs reflected in plate steel,
Lurching towards a devolution referendum.
As we overcame the crest of Lanarkshire
The valley rolled successive folds below
With smoky chimneys and repeating waves
Of urban sprawl, high rise stacks and factories
Sealed securely to let none in.
I leaned my forehead against the glass
Peering down towards the river
Marked only by the lowest line

The eye could reach amidst the concrete mass.
This city gave me birth and hope,
Here to return and cast a vote.
As we began the downward climb
The bus began to fill with folk.
Two miners from the Welfare,
A woman going to shop in town,
Youngsters on their way to disco
And a head-scarved gaggle fresh from bingo.
Suddenly he was up into the aisle
No longer dozing by my shoulder,
But towering to the rooflights
Leaflets flourished in his hands from nowhere.
'Have you voted yet today?
Ladies, it's your parliament at stake.
Scotland's right belongs to you as well.
Aye, look around you, lads,
Nationless, the workers' cause unwon.
For King and country, mam?
I fought to beat the fascists,
Now I want to win the peace,
For us and for the nations of the world.'
He had the bus alight and laughing.
Then he set them singing,
Clydeside red, the weavers' ballads,
Polaris and the CND, with bawdy numbers in between
Then unexpectedly the bus arrived.
'Jesus Christ,' the driver spat contentedly,
'Will you be on my shift the morn?'
Men shook his hand, women hugged.
'God,' he said, 'But I could use a drink.'

Four

Are ye drinkin, big man?
Aye, don't mind if Ah dae.
Slainte.
Whit were ye in?
51st Highland! Goan wi ye, a dodger.
Mussolini's surrender in yer troosers?
Stick tae the beer, man
An keep yer flies buttoned up.
Jesus Christ, ah see it noo.
Aye, Ah believe ye, big yin, calm doon.
Fuck me, the place is crawlin wi Tallies.
Demob? The toon's heavin, Argyll Street tae the Broomielaw
Aff the boats an ontae the trains.
Pair bastarts, the whures are aa buggered
Back tae the yairds, fur me.
Hoos aboot yersel?
Gathering sangs? Whit kin o work's thon?
Scotland's sangs? Fuckin hell.
Aye that'll be right. Oan the British Broadcastin Corporation.
Winston Churchill an the Philharmonic Orchestra?
No fur the likes o me.
Ma rent's paid tae Glesca Corporation
That auld stuff's feenished noo
Wi the war an that,
Is that no right, big yin?
Ah mind oan ma mammy singing,
'The Flooers o the Forest
Are aa wede awa'

Yours tae? Fuck me.
They're awa noo onyroads.
The boys liked a singsong but
Who do ye think made the D Day dodgers?
That's a gallus wan tae collect.
Are ye drinkin, big man?
Aye, don't mind if Ah dae.

Five

Old bones lie light and restless through a summer night
So early in the morning I was on the beach
Walking carefully along the wrack, prodding now and then
Upturned kindling or a shell complete or something new and
    unforeseen
Gulls looped overhead, the sun threw discs of golden light
White breakers rolled and crashed onto the shore
Like runners who have raced a thousand miles of open sea.
Sandy tore around in foaming circles at the racers' feet.
My mind was on the war that broke my old man's sleep
With memories of death and butchered flesh, gas
Choking at our throats and chest. Local men
Whose bodies sank in Flanders' mud or deep below the sea.
Eye catches a tall dark figure on the edge
Coming round the bay, nearer with each long loose stride.
I clamped the battered hat more firmly to my head
And focused as a giant stripling topped with short black hair
    approached.
Sandy went wild with friendly yelps and leaps of introduction
But something recognised, cheap spectacles at tilt, the jaunty
    moustache.

This is where Odysseus was washed ashore, his naked body
    caked with brine.
But when the local girls came with the dawn to wash and play,
Odysseus rose a grimy gnarled lion, a branch before his privates.
Nausicaa the princess stood her ground to welcome him.
Perhaps she saw the lines of strength and beauty beneath his grey
    and tangled mane.
We laughed, no need for commentary, and he threw his rucksack
    to the ground

The clothes went next, stripped off into a bundle on the sand
And in he went splashing and careering, the dog his mad familiar
Long white legs and lanky sunburnt arms, a penis waving.
He breasted waves with screams of anguish and delight.
I kicked off my boots, rolled up the trouser legs
To let the wavelets trickle round my horny feet.
He tumbled out with glistening water like dew upon his pure
    lithe flesh.

When he was dry I offered breakfast but his gaze was set.
A lot of places still to reach, his journey down the coast
Was prelude to a European summer even as it darkened to
    another storm.
So I watched him stretching out, a lonely traveller on the strand
But sunlight seemed to glance along the sea to follow,
And green hills rose to surround the sand
And welcome a host of drifting wanderers returned.
I blinked and turned towards the long trail back upriver.

Citadels

Citadels

One

The High Street like a spine
gives structure to the Town
backbone of streets and houses
hard resilient walls
Craigleith quarried
north-wind scoured
sea-salted burgh of the Scots.
No shadow play of memory here
but light etched on a grey shield
badges that do not betray.
We hold our knowledge close
and keep our own dead company.
The red-stained floor at Holyrood
and Mary's bosom soaked with Rizzio's blood;
Charlie holding Highland Court –
graceful plaids and dancing crests
oblivious of Culloden's final harvest.
The balcony of Moray House where Argyle
looked disdainful down to see the Graham ride to his death,
till two years later Campbell Mor
goes the same way to his dust.
They lie now in St Giles, opposing tombs,
but always on Montrose's heart a red rose lies.
Up on, past Parliament Square,
an auld sang ended, to the Castle Rock
the Crown of Scotland where eye bejewelled bedazzled
gazes on the pilgrim's prize
relics of our nationhood.

Two

Number: One, Three?
Platonic Root, Magic Flute? the Morning Bus
with music piped upstairs
seductions of the mass.
Professor, take your seat to scan
the printed front, the naked man
the times review,
does everybody stare like you?

Eternal city of the crude warm flesh,
a shapeless overall
with weight of hungry mouths.
In her slippers dry Aristotle
takes his lunchtime stroll
propounds the matter and the form for all who seek
a university town.
His face screwed tight, a work of years,
to lecture on the democratic boobs:
the Greeks are always Greeks,
my boy, the trogs are trogs;
body bears the imprint of the mind.

The proper study of mankind is men?
Protagoras said it first
(bon mots are in dispute) but which?
Artist, anatomist and lover,
Leonardo was all three.
Professor, let your eyes roam up and down the spines,
sip your evening wine.
You've got them every way,
next year they'll ask you to the USA.

Three

Dream-spanned Kosmo
bulging in the coat of many colours
skyways from your fingers radiate
around the globe. Stars jerk like puppets.
Your smile lights up a thousand vistas.
If you raised your spangled topper
you would sail into the ether
like a great striped balloon.

Flight two-six-seven-o
parting, parting
flight departing

From the fifth floor
on the bridge I saw
poised between the concrete frames
of entrance and of exit,
your hair waving

One morning
when I got to summer
and met you
the quiet pattern of the leaves
the way your hair fell.

Flight two-six-seven-o
parting, parting
flight departing

But Mr President (forgive my levity
I speak for all humanity)
your power has linked whole continents in one,
benefits too great for me to numerate
one state one wealth one world corporate.

I'll wait at flight arrival
two-six-seven-o
Don't be late

From San Francisco take the Silver Streak.
If you lost me at the Mardi Gras watch for my gesticulation.

Flight 2670
parting parting

Restless threads
to weave a moment in a thousand dreams
we tossed upon the magic carpet
rolled together and apart

Flight departing

You like me
you listen to me
you hold out your breasts

I thought you were –
Rotating on the escalator
on and on glass agape
echoing corridors
littered lounges
shuttling buses
empty runways
I love –

Flight departed, parted

Thank you.
Click.
You

Four

Perfect assertion
blank unseeing beauty
you terrify myself
hewed from the glacier's face
and trapped to vindicate
the pose of form
and the body's season.

Constructed in your ribs
down to your flanks and buttocks
I see a perfect section
but suspended there
a restless motion
like the bark
twisted on the surface
of a spawning sea.

Bored by the sacrifices
sceptical of prowess
we take you from the glens
and set you in this empty hall
while I sit hunched, perplexed
my only clue the pain
the dawning radiance
in your belly.

Five

When Pharaoh built his pyramids
the people groped in line.
He wound them round his aspirations
and built them slab by slab
into a monument.

They fumbled with their discontent
but had no concept
other than the concrete
fact of Pharaoh
mounting step by step
on tiers of bodies
to be their God.

But Pharaoh feared flood and drought
and was oppressed by plenty.
He counted every bushel
and broke his sleep
to dream of straw held back
of people building
with their own bricks.

Six

i

Miss Tokyo girl
in western style,
transfixed between the old and new
accumulated memories
like destination stickers,
you recall a photograph
so bright and perfectly presented
waving goodbye.

ii

Framed at the window
the minister's wife
her look the courage
of the gently worn down
a portrait in the drawing room
she sits at night
embroidering the fall.

iii

Her breasts swing in focus,

from one mud hovel to the next

resting place,

a child strapped on back

its bony feet aslant like fins.

Beneath the scrub

the camera cannot go

but scratching in the earth

you smelt survival.

The men are cleaning guns

instead of wells

A week of sweet water?

spitting blood in the sand.

Tusitala

Tusitala

for Robert Louis Stevenson, 1997

Mixing a salad
on the verandah
home-grown lettuce
parsley chives
a slice of South Seas squash
sea-salt and earth pepper,
olive oil for France
and for the Scots,
aye vinegar –
Vailima dressing.
The wine uncorked
from Burgundy
and breathing air
it has Samoan rights
to breathe.
'Do I look strange?'
hands to his head,
life support switched off
the theatre goes dark.

Images re-run on the eye,
hands lean and brown
quick-moving leaves
trunk pent and slender
its spirit a strung bow
ready for release,
frail rich-tinted flesh
brown eyes
curved nose and mobile mouth
intent on mixing

sensual and critical,
sexed for men and women,
presiding over wine and salad.
Did concentration evaporate,
or close its eyes
against the dazzle of reality?

'To have lived in the light
of that splendid life
that beautiful being
only to see it
from one moment to the next
converted into a fable,
a thing that has been
and has ended.'
The story peters out ...
dictating from scant notes
even this morning
he never faltered for a word
but gave out the sentences
as clearly and steadily
as if reading
from an unseen book.

Unfinished absence
to be haunting
the same moment.

Fables have their own time
island entertainments
or fragments of embodied life
refractions light and dark
recoverings
of race and memory
passionate elusive by-blows
of a richer being.

But roots are intertwined
of ghostly self and buried flesh;
the bodied life is geography and race
though richer than the blood
the common pulse of memory
and imagination
to signify the human.

This road is not a fable –
ala loto, loving heart –
and on it Lewis
you came home,
Laird of Samoa,
all night the chiefs
watched by your couch
while forty men cut and slashed
a path up to the mountain.
No stranger's hand touched
your interlocking fingers
in the form of prayer
a community bore you
to the grave
under a star-filled sky
glad did you live
and gladly die
laid down with a will.

Tusitala
your consciousness their spirit
freely given
your flesh their body,
the lighthouse builders
are Samoan now
and Vaea's mountain children
fruits of your strange fertility.
This is how the burden

was discharged
holding ancestors in trust
not letting them miscarry,
but giving them a family
and a nation,
Scotland still cannot accept.
no final monument,
unburied here
the dreamer and the exile
inhabiting the lonely muir
and the peewit calling.

'Tracts of the land
are desolate,
you go for miles
and meet no one
smoking hearth
only sheep feeding
on moors and glens
peopled once
as you are peopled,
the Gaels of Alba cleared
to every corner of the earth
except their own'
you do not speak lightly
because you love Samoa
'I have chosen it
to be my home
while I live
and my grave
after I am dead,
and I love the people
I have chosen
to be laid down
where they die.

And I see a day of great battle
the last and the great
opportunity
by which it will be decided
whether you will pass away
as so many clans and races
have gone into the dreamtime
or standfast
to give your children
a living landscape
you received in gift.'

Tusitala, storyteller
your prophecy comes home,
at last
no mausoleum on a hill,
a road to build
for everyone who chooses
Scot life-embodied
land.

Jamie Stewart's
Return to Edinburgh

Jamie Stewart's Return to Edinburgh

The Port lies open to my Majestie
Long life, good health, prosperitie
The people's benison.
Ma airse sair scaddit wi this saddle
'Oh why should London only see thee shine
Is not the Forth as well as Thameside thine?
Though London vaunt she has more wealth in store,
Let it suffice that Forth doth love thee more.'

Once I took pleasure in the muse
Now I governe with my pen
One stroke and it is done
What thousands by the sword could not secure.

'See, Majestie, upon this Port
Your arms and effigy displayed
Beatis pacifici: the words of peace.
Two countries you have joined
And ended strife's long emnitie
You are a Gate between two nations
United through a single monarchie.'

Neitherbow, the Warld's End
ayont lie English and the wolves.

'*Jacobus Rex, Anna Regina*,
Carved to remember
Your sacred Majestie's deliverance
From the conspiracie of England,
Gunpowder, Treason and Plot.'
Pair Annie all but blawn tae smithereens
wi me an the bairns at Parliament.

'We thank our loyal citizens of Edinburgh.'

A Traitor's Gate erectit
fur aa wha ettle tae kill a king
murder maist foul tae raise a haund
agin the Lord's anointit.
Traitors gangin backwards at the horse's tail,
heids soused in glaur,
their privvy pairts excisit and brunt
afore the nebs o the unworthily begot.
Bowels an hert are coupit oot,
the heids wha hatchit hackit aff
an aa the members o the body
portioned tae be publicly exposit,
sweitmait tae corbies an tae gulls.

'Oh Majestie that came of warlike state
Who even in your mother's womb
Was prey to cruel and violent men
Should yet possess amitie abundant
To sheathe the swords of Christendom.
Borne on this golden globe
I am an angel of the heavenly skies
Here are the keys of this city,
You shall have the power to do to us
Whatever justice and law suggest.'

'I your Sovereign take these keys.'
Luik at her haurd wee pappies
prickin tits in the cauld.
When Annie cam tae Edinburgh
they gied her a Bible wi the keys
but she's a papist still.

'We hae orderit a new bell, Majestie,
Fur the steiple o The Neitherbow
Senatus populusque Edinburgensi'
Aye nae doot the cooncil an rabble conjoined.

But whit o Caesar Imperator?
'What motto is emblazoned, Baillie,
on the Bell? *Nemo me impune lacessit.*'
The auld Scots seickness.
Wha daur meddle wi me.
Cuddies wi'oot the reign o reason.
'And *Soli Deo Gloria*, Majestie.'
'Aye, God be praisit, Baillie,
Kingship is the gift of God alane.'

'O gracious Lord and mighty prince,
Sheba to your Solomon,
I longed to come to you,
Not to bear precious gifts
But to enjoy your wisdom
That the whole world talks of.'

Oh Sheba of the southern Nile
Give me a sign of love
A gift of balsam from your Afric clime
Consort with me to taste the joy
Of those who drink from Pallas' breasts –

'Haud ticht at the reins, Majestie,
She's pooin at the mooth.'
'Aye, Baillie, let us proceed
With decorum up the Hie Street.'

'Pass not by without a glance,
For on this gracious house
is graven a text
Luve God abune all and your neibour as yersel.'

Mosman's hoose at the heid o the bow,
Mosman wha wrocht the crown
that hung aboot ma heid
e'en as a bairn. Mosman,
Gowdsmith, Cooncillor an Deacon o the Craft.
He denied ma richt tae rule

'And we that is Trades
Pray long life and prosperitie
To your royal Majestie
To defend your sacred persone
Even unto daith.'

'Thank you loyal trades and crafts of Edinburgh.'

He stole ma croun intae the castle,
fur that he wis condemnit,
pit tae the horn, his gear roupit,
his hoose forfeit tae the King.
An when his treacherie wis dune
Mosman wis hurlit backwards frae a cairt
passed his ain hoose tae hing
at the Mercat Cross till deid.
His heid spiked oan the Castle wa
fur bein loyal tae ma mither,
Mary ma mither in England.

'In the troubled times Majestie,
Of your late mother, the Queen,
Master John Knox dwelt here
An gave up his godly soul
In the hands o the Most High'

Aye the cantin tribe wha abusit her
while Mosman deed tae defend her
the sacred person, the wame,
that cairrit me intae life;
the breists that gied me sook
till I wis torn awa,
no like my Annie's bairns,
an orphan king. Ma faither deid
blawn tae smithereens, ma mither waur
gien up tae whuredom,
an me wioot a sister or a brither,
yet monarch o this realm
forbye the heir tae England,
whaur she wis gaun tae bide
till lyfe endit, Mither.
Mammie, I never kenned you.

'Majestie, your Scottish Parliament awaits'
'Gang forrit, Baillie, tae the ploy.'

Light Assembly
on Calton Hill

Light Assembly on Calton Hill
A Millennium Peformance Poem

Fire on the mountain, light on the hill
Gainst castle rock the clouds are breaking
North winds blow freedom from the sea.

Panorama from the hill of old and new, firth and sky
Down dark closes, up terraced streets, fisherman and city gent
Workers, lawyers, beggars, actors all in painter's eye
White wash of sun, a camera shutters close to see the light.

Fire on the mountain, light on the hills
Gainst castle rock the clouds are breaking
North winds blow freedom from the sea.

Stippled cityscape of stone, towers and steeples
Concepts in time, ideas of being, human liberty, equality
For aw that brought crashing down the pillars of destruction
Till monuments of war give way to parliaments of peace.

Fire on the mountain, light on the hill
Gainst castle rock the clouds are breaking
North winds blow freedom from the sea.

Mind goes deeper faster than a spinning axis
Gravity of planets gyre electric energy
Shake the kaleidoscope into its firework-coloured theatre
Light shifts across the universe now wave now particle in flight.

Fire on the mountain, light on the hill
Gainst castle rock the clouds are breaking
North winds blow freedom from the sea.

It all works together if we only can connect
Earth's story fired in fossil layers, the living cell
The helix gene that codes disease and healing power
This city's spirit and the body of its folk.

Fire on the mountain, light on the hill
Gainst castle rock the clouds are breaking
North winds blow freedom from the sea.

To the Hill

To the Hill

Symphony for Holyrood

One

andante

Early light to dusk
blanket haared or lucent lensed
on slopes and troughs and rocks
lonely runners
pounding out their beats
wearing down on time worn tracks
single yet in consort dogged to break free.
A common ground to pattern steep and crag
night and day in every weather
till as bird flights criss-cross in season
the hill is flagged with gaudy balloons
soaring kites and billowing marquees.
Light moment of release to drift
above the rocky flanks and scarcely feel
the indentation, no vestige of a beginning
no prospect of an end in moving mass
unmeasured by the individual footfall,
all work is turned to play.
Of these interludes the hill retains
no mark or memory, blows away to sea.
Persistently the folk resume to run
walk or climb unobtrusive to the summit
small scale paths thread through
the wider element, space between
the earth and sky
being air.

Two

adagio

On the hill in every weather
no two hours alike air in motion,
cloud form dampening smoothing
steady soak of rain, bake of sun,
the scar of wind and hail,
or mantling of the pure white snow.
The hill is veined by hidden routes,
springs and streams between beds of rock,
seeps out the boggy gathering
to dam, drain to lochs.
Beneath each shifting water
tone of vegetation, the latent build
in sweeping crags, bony ribs and outcrops
around the cumulated hump of strength
deceptively worn down, resurgent
in new light to mount and crest.

On the lowest gentle slopes a sandstone
palace nestles with coned towers and gardens.
From St Margaret's Well the intricate
stone weaving traces rise
above the ancient seat of royal parliament and power,
stone to memorialise a sacred cross
and for a time endure.
Along the track another sandstone growth
St Anthony's light looks out to sea
a beacon crumbling above the loch
on which swans glide and wheel in ordered grace
to lift wing westward, Tir nan Og
where faithful spirits are forever free.

The shoulder of the hill turns always seawards,
climb sunwise round the flanks to think and walk,
till Dunsapie and the lion's peak appear
ringed with terraces, the spiral markings
ramparts rubbed away, and undersides
of homesteads like upturned boats
cooried down beneath the storm.
Human habitation eroding centuries restore
to the hill without demur or degradation.
Wind ripples through the pass of shadows
a shiver on the upper loch
between the summits guardians
watch you like herons in the reeds,
stony spirits till they flap disturbed
languorously away, intent on quiet fishing.

Three

scherzo

Sidestep in time
    history's dance
on Arthur's Seat
    beacons blaze
the fabled king
    rides south to war
shieldwall Saxon
    bloodied red
before day's dawn
    Celtic lament
at Tref-yr-Lyn
    swords in the lake
between deershorns
    sign of the cross
Margaret's relics
    Haly Rude
sair sanct for the crown
    David's gift
Kingdom of Scots
    siege perilous
Scots wha hae
    Bannockburn
Royal Hunting Park
    Stewart dynasty
Reine de France
    Queen of Scots
Thrie Estaites
    John Commonweill

move up Jock
    Jamie the Saxt
gie us a break
    civil wars
gang tae the muir
    gallows tree
Act of Union
    parcel o rogues
the Stuart's return
    redcoat walls
hey Johnnie Cope
    Charlie's awa
British Empire
    radical road
Regina Vic
    Tartan trews
war memorial
    hill of the dead
begin again
    Holyrood.

Four

finale, moderato

The landward light goes down
by birkie braes and broom
till sheen of water opens, wavering dusk,
ringed by trees and leafy terrace,
mirror of the sun and moon,
beneath Kirk Tower of Duddingston.
Chalicing the streams and hidden springs
a sanctuary place invites your offering
swords cast in the lake, bread on the waters.
Each season brings you back
to contemplate what changes
yet continues as before.

Leave something of yourself,
go on to close the circle
by Wells o Wearie beneath St Leonard's Bank,
you reach again to Holyrood's surprise
a Scottish Parliament uprisen.
Gateway for those returning from the hill,
completes a Royal Mile in civic stone.
The crested roofs look out to sea
or fix a watchful eye towards the castle.
From the rectangular back border
forms splay and curve in each direction
wrapping Queensberry House around
where landed dynasts hatched the union.
Then granite blocks mass upward
bearing the debating chamber in their thrust,
an oaken pageant beamed with light.

Above this ensemble still the line
of Calton Hill, democracy's cairns and columns
memorialise war and peace.
This is the lowest point of ground
founded in springs and streams
the building leans towards land and sea
islands of the firth and beacon heights
beneath the shifting lightful sky,
air earth water fire assemble
a Scottish gathering, place and folk
in common purpose, the chorale
to lift our voices to the hill.

A Song for Scotland

A Song for Scotland
To 'Highland Cathedral'

Land of the mountain, islands and the sea,
Highland and Lowland, that gives life to me,
Mother of justice and humanity,
Be our last refuge, stronghold of the free.
Be our last refuge stronghold of the free

Scotland, to you our minds and spirits soar.
Lift our eyes homeward and our sight restore.
Guide all earth's restless children safe ashore.
Shine light to humankind for evermore.
Shine light to humankind for evermore

Land of the mountain, islands and the sea,
Highland and Lowland, that gives life to me,
Source of the strength and love always to be
From start to journey's end faithful to thee.
From start to journey's end faithful to thee

Cradle King

Preface to Cradle King

CRADLE KING IS A dramatic poem for one actor, and a skull manipulated by the actor. The part was first played by Robin Thomson at The Netherbow Theatre, Edinburgh in August 2003. The author would like to acknowledge the contribution of Robin Thomson's improvisation skills to the final version.

In 1603 James VI of Scotland also became James I of England and moved to London, returning to Scotland only once in a long reign. Soon after his arrival in England James became the patron of Shakespeare's theatre company, now rechristened 'The King's Men'. In the fifteen nineties, and again in 1601, Shakespeare's colleague Laurence Fletcher had toured to Scotland and performed under the patronage of James at Holyrood and in a specially constructed theatre in Blackfriars Wynd, just across from The Netherbow. James remained, throughout his life, a passionate patron and practitioner of the arts, particularly literature and theatre.

Although a successful ruler by the standards of his time, James never emotionally outgrew the horrors of his troubled childhood. Having survived an assassination attempt in his mother's womb the infant James was later to learn of his father's murder, in which his mother Mary, Queen of Scots, may have been complicit. His mother was then imprisoned, deposed and forced into exile, leaving James at the mercy of the Scottish nobility and of his tutor George Buchanan – a brilliant man of letters – then in crabby old age.

James may have been bi-sexual and his close teenage friendship with Esmée Stuart was brutally broken up by a jealous court. When James married it was to a Danish Princess Anne who was also mad about theatre. However, despite raising a large family of future kings and queens (including the ill-fated Charles I and his son James VII and II) marriage brought James more strife and unease and, in his old age, he seemed an isolated almost Lear-like figure. The connections between Shakespeare's great tragedies and James' biography were first suggested by Professor Thomas Riis of Odense University and Arthur Melville Clark.

This drama is presented with special thanks to William Shakespeare who hereby finally returns the favour of King James' artistic patronage.

King   Horsie, horsie
Clip-clop, clip-clop
Trot, horsie, trot
[*He begins to tap out the rhythm on his armrest*]
Faster, horsie, faster
[*trotting rhythm*]
Gang speedie
Speedie gang
[*quicker*]
Ride-a-cock-horsie
Ride-a-cock-horsie
[*building*]
We're fleein, horsie
Fleein
Ride-a-cock-horsie
Ride-a-cock-horsie
Tally ho!
Ride-a-cock-horsie
Loose the dugs
The dugs gang fleein
[*beating a gallop*]
Drive it doon, drive it doon
Ride-a-cock-horse
Ride-a-cock-horse
Spear the belly
Please, aye, please, spear the belly
Drive it doon, bluidy spear
Gralloch in the guts,
Please bitch, gralloch
[*rhythm breaks down*]
Ride-a-cock-horsie
Aye, ride, horsie, ride.

The heid's aff noo
an I'll no wear the horns.
Dr Fian's the horny god.
Let him play the devil.
Lap my antlered limbs at last.
Warm my legs in the bluidy entrails
Succour, siccar; crookit, straucht.
You filthy wee bastart
I'll tan yer hide fur ye.
Piteous Jesus, no again.
I'll be aricht noo.
Please, be composed.
It was just that play upset me.
Seeing it all again, as if it had come true.
There was nothing like that
when I was wee in Scotland.
There were tales and sangs for bairns.
And Maister Buchanan, wha is, who was my
      dominie,
Wrote plays in Latin.
Not shadows of the night.
'Show.
Show.
Aye, show his eyes and grieve his heart.
Come like shadows then depart.'
The ministers were right after all.
It's the devil's art. Satan's Man,
The Player King. Chase them oot,
lock, stock and barrel.
No, I'm not ganging tae bed.
Let me alane. I'm bound tae masel.
I'll sit here by the fire
and see pictures in the flame

till the night visions give me peace.
Puir Jamie, puir wee laddie
[*strokes the skull*]

Skull   That which serves and seeks for gain
and follows but for form
will pack when it begins to rain
and leave thee in the storm.
Door Jamie's a cold.
Cover him up, poor naked wretch.
Unaccommodated man is no more
but such a poor bare forked animal
as thou art unbuttoned here.

King   They flattered me like a dog
and told me I had the white hairs in my beard
ere the black ones were there.
When the rain came to wet me once,
and the wind to make me chatter,
there I found them, there I smelt em out.

Skull   Our flesh and blood my lord is grown so vile
that it doth hate what gets it.

King   Blow, winds, and crack your cheeks! Rage, blow.
You cataracts and hurricanes spout
till you have drenched our steeples, drowned the
    cocks.
Crack nature's moulds all germens spill at once
That makes ingrateful man.

Skull   O nuncle, court holy water in a dry house
is better than this rain water out o' door.
Good nuncle, in and ask thy sons' blessing.
Here's a night pities neither wise men nor fools.

King   Rumble thy bellyful; spit fire, spout rain.
Nor rain, wind, thunder, fire are my sons
I tax not you, you elements, with unkindness.
I never gave you kingdom, called you children.
You owe me no subscriptions.

Skull   He that has a house to put's head in has a good
       headpiece.
The codpiece that will house before the head has any,
the head and he shall louse.
The man that makes his toe
what his crown should seem
shall of a corn cry woe
and turn his sleep to wake –

King   A dream, a dream, the king wakes!
Sleep is broken.

Skull   Tell the laddie a story, a tale, tae soothe him an
       solace him.
Aye, puir mitherless bairn that he is.

King   Once upon a time, there was a king and he had
three fine sons, three princes. So the king decided to
share out their inheritance, and to live with each of
them in turn.
But first of all, he decided to ask them a question.
So he says to the first boy, 'How much do you love
me?'
And he said, 'Father, I love you as much as all the
gold and silver in the kingdom.'
'Very good,' said the king. 'And what about you?'
he asked the next boy. 'Father,' said the second
prince, 'I love you as much as all the gems and
jewels in the world.'

'Very good,' said the king. 'I like that answer.'
'Now,' he says to the youngest son, his favourite,
'how much do you love me, my boy?'
But the youngest prince was sensible and honest and
he said, 'Father, I love you more than salt.'
'Salt!' says the king, astonished, 'What nonsense is
that – common salt. You don't love me at all.' He
felt a fool in front of all his courtiers.
'From this day on you are banished from my
kingdom. Never show your face here again.'
So the young boy fled and became a servant in a
neighbouring kingdom. And the old king, he went to
stay with each of his remaining sons in turn.
But he wasn't really happy and the two princes
became less and less polite to the old man. Now
they had the money and the power, they felt that he
was in their way and they ignored everything he
said. Soon the kingdom was in a mess. The princes
fell out with all their neighbours and trade ceased.
Everything was in short supply, even salt.
Now the youngest prince heard about the shortages
and he decided to bring some food to his old father,
and some salt to season it. Of course, the boy was
dressed like a servant so no-one knew him.
The old king was wasting away in his bedchamber,
mumbling over the fire. He had no stomach for even
the little food he was given, since it had no savour.
All his interest in life was gone.
So the boy went straight to the palace kitchen and
put salt in his father's broth, and took it up to the
chamber. And he put a spoonful to his father's
mouth and, when the old king supped, his face lit up

and he drained the bowl, and revived. He came back
to life and recognised his son.
'Oh, my dear boy,' the old king said, 'now I
understand. You love me more than salt.'
[*The King is falling asleep*]
So the youngest prince was restored to his
inheritance. He was set over the two brothers and
ruled wisely in accordance with his father's good
advice.
Isn't that a ... nice ... story?

Ghost	Aye, Jamesie, still sleepin are you? Indulging the senses yet again. But your time's almost feenished, Jamesie. You'll fall in ice and then in fire. You'll be wracked by gout, and then you'll be deid. Dead, Jamesie, within two years and ripe tae meet your maker. You evil little son of Belial, wake up. [*The King comes to with a start, his childhood stammer returns at start of speech*]
King	Dominie! No, no, dinna beat me.
Ghost	It's time for your parritch, majestie. But have you done your Greek translation yet? Plutarch before parritch, Jamesie.
King	No, dominie, but I made a poem last night.
Ghost	A poem, did you? In Latin, Greek, or English?
King	It's in Scots, dominie.
Ghost	Scots, is it? Verra guid. Weel, maister, hie doon tae yer breakfast

and then we'll hae the poem soonded oot.
But neist time, mind,
I'll pare yer arse fur ye
if ye dinna pairse yer Greek.

King   Aye dominie.
[*follows ghost with his eyes*]
Aye, get oot, ye auld bastart.
I'm king now, and you can't touch me.
I'm a sacred person.
Get out of my vision.
Go and slaver in your smelly old beard.
I've got Will Shakespeare and Ben Jonson for my
    poets now.
I don't need you, smelly old bard.
You're full of worm's droppings now anyway.
[*to skull*] I telt him, didn't I? Buchanan.
    [*no response*]
Aye well, he had no right to beat me.
I was a king even then, a cradle king.
Mind he was a master poet – a makar.
He made me a prentice in the divine arts
and he spoke his poetry out loud
the way that words should sing,
in whatever tongue.
The English maul their Greek and Latin
with bad pronunciation. As for their Scots,
the dominie and I are baith scunnered.
Tis true I am a cradle king
yet doe remember everything
that I have heretofore put·out
and yet begin not for to doubt.
To doubt even masel, my royal self.

Ghost   Time for your Scripture, Jamesie.

King   Is it?

Ghost   Aye. What's the chapter?

King   I dinna ken.

Ghost   Aye you dae.

King   Dinna.

Ghost   Aye you dae!
Gie us the chapter, Jamesie.
You do remember every thing.

King   The Gospel according to Matthew at the fourteenth
chapter and reading from the first verse. Hear the
word of the Lord.
At that time Herod heard of the fame of Jesus. And
he said unto his servants, 'This is John the Baptist
risen from the dead; and therefore mighty works do
show forth themselves in him.'
For Herod had laid hold on John and bound him
and put him in prison for Herodias' sake, his
brother Philip's wife. For John said unto him, 'It is
not lawful for you to have her.'
[*The King begins to get more involved in the story.*]
And when he would have put him to death he feared
the multitude because they counted him as a
prophet.
But when Herod's birthday was kept, the daughter
of Herodias
[*danced by skull as breast*] danced before them
[*hums music, sniffs breast*] and pleased Herod.
[*King is pleased*]
Whereupon he promised with an oath

78

to give Salome whatever she would ask.
And she, being instructed of her mother, said
'Give me here John Baptist's head on a charger.'
And the king was sorry. [*King is not sorry*]
Nevertheless for the oath's sake and them which sat
with him at meat, he commanded it to be given her.
And he sent and beheaded John in the prison.
[*Breast is now skull on hand*]
and his head was brought in a charger and given to
the damsel and she brought it to her mother.
Thanks be to God for this reading of His Holy
Word, Amen.

Skull	I felt a right tit doing that.
Ghost	What's the lesson of the Scripture, Jamesie? Come on, out loud.
King	Evil tyrants must be slain.
Ghost	That's right, Jamesie, and what else?
King	Don't marry within the forbidden degrees.
Ghost	... especially ...
King	... especially within the blood royal.
Ghost	Good. Anything else?
King	Aye, don't lay violent hands on the Lord's anointed.
Ghost	No, the Lord's Prophet suffers persecution in the cause of righteousness.
King	But the evil in the land must be cut off.
Ghost	Especially the royal evil, Jamesie, cut off at the neck.

King   That's enough, Buchanan, you've gone too far.
I am monarch of three kingdoms now.
Get back in the shadows
and stop your treasonable mouth
with your own filth.
The right of Kings reigns supreme
conferred by God alone.
You've paddled your dirty fingers
in a Queen's blood.
She was my mother.

Ghost   She wis a whure, Jamesie,
an a murderess like Herodias.
The snake deserves to die.

King   Get away.
Else I'll put you to the rack.

Ghost   Dinnae fret, laddie. I'm going.
But I think, ma wee mannie,
that the boot's really on the ither foot.

[*Ghost fades, laughing, leaving King in tears*]

Skull   It's alright, Jamesie, he's gone.

King   I don't read his plays anyway,
John the Baptist. No-one bothers with it now.
Shakespeare's the man,
and he's written a Scottish play for me.
That's more than you ever did, dominie.
The Player's King is also King of Scots.
A poisoned chalice if ever there was one.
I used to hang over the castle ramparts at Stirling,
and look north into wastelands of marsh and
mountain. Bogs, papists and savages.

'That's the Lennox,' dominie would say, sneaking up
behind me. 'That is – was – your royal father's
country. The Scots are a people of ancient lineage
and custom. They speak Erse. I, of course, speak
Erse and am writing the History of the Scottish
Nation.'
Nation my airse! Reivers and heathens, beyond
civility or true religion. If you don't believe me
watch Shakespeare's play – the Scottish one.
Now I govern Scotland with my pen, at a safe
distance. Politic. One stroke and it is done, what
thousands by the sword failed to achieve. Aye, or a
sgian dhu in the kidneys.
Macbeth, your Lady was a witch,
a handmaid of Satan gave your children suck.
False Queen, and mistress of the night.
[*The King is attracted by this idea.*]
The raven himself is hoarse ...

Skull   Caw.

King   That croaks the fatal entrance under my
             battlements.
         Come, you spirits that tend on mortal thoughts,
         unsex me here
         and fill me, from the crown to the toe, top full
         of direst cruelty. Come to my woman's breasts
         and take my milk for gall, you murdering ministers.
         Come thick night and pall thee in the dimmest
             smoke of hell
         that my keen knife see not the wound it makes
         nor heaven peep through the blanket of the dark
         to cry 'Hold, hold.'
         Aye, Shakespeare kens hoo tae please.

Skull Just a minute.
     We will proceed no further in this business.
     He hath honoured me of late and I have bought
       golden opinions from all sorts of people.

King Was the hope drunk, wherein you dressed yourself?
     Hath it slept since? And wakes now to look so green
       and pale
     at what it did so freely. From this time
     such I account thy love. Art thou afraid
     to be the same in act and valour
     as thou art in desire?

King I have given suck and know
     how tender is to love the babe that milks me.

     [*Skull becomes breast, then baby*]

     I would, while it was smiling in my face,
     have plucked my nipple from his gums
     and dashed his brains out had I so sworn
     as you have done to this.
     Mummy I never knew you
     but I believe you wrocht
     tae preserve me in life.
     I go and it is done. The bell invites me.
     Hear it not, Darnley, for it is a knell
     that summons thee to heaven or to hell.

Skull Yeh, he tried to murder you, an all.

King Had he not resembled
     my father as he slept I had done it.
     My husband,
     go get some water
     and wash this filthy witness from your hand.

Why did you bring these daggers from the place?
They must lie there. Go carry them and smear
the sleeping grooms with blood.

Skull   Not as daft as you look, are you?.

[Pause. The King becomes a King again.]

King   We have scotched the snake not killed it.
She'll close and be herself, whilst our poor malice
remains in danger of her former tooth.
But let the frame of things disjoint, both the worlds
suffer,
ere we will eat our meal in fear, and sleep
in the affliction of these terrible dreams
that shake us nightly. Better be with the dead
whom we, to gain our peace, have sent to peace,
than on the torture of the mind to lie
in restless ecstasy. Darnley is in his grave.
After life's fitful fever, he sleeps well.
Treason has done his worst. Nor steel, nor poison,
Malice, domestic, foreign levy, nothing
can touch him further.

Skull   Mummy, Daddy, where are you?
Show, show?

King   Aye show. Will the line stretch out to the crack of
doom?
And some the treble sceptres carry?
Now I see tis true
the blood-boltered Banquo smiles upon me
and points at them, for mine!

Skull   There's the Scots for you,
ferrets in a sack.
And that's a happy ending, is it?

King   When I was in my mother's womb
they tried to drag me out,
a bloodied foetus.
My father Darnley murdered
before I could be weaned.
At five I saw my Grandpa Lennox
killed before my eyes.
Twice I was kidnapped,
my life hanging by a thread.
They took away the lovely Esmée,
my heart's first friend.
They would have killed him if they could.
And the other one, the devil's helper,
stood in my own bedchamber
with a drawn blade.
Keep away, Bothwell,
you're dead and in your grave in Denmark.
No Danish ghost can haunt me here.
My boys are safe
and on a British throne.
I'll never let them suffer
what I had to grue.
Kingship is the gift of God alone
and everyone will bend their necks
because it is God's will.
The Welsh, the Irish, and the Scots
yoked to the State Imperial.
No surrender to chaos or to dissolution.
Our souls and bodies
must be governed.
Never stain your crown.
I would not be cruel, bairns,

I would not be cruel
but they must obey.
They must confess their fault.
We use the gentler tortures first,
Proceeding, gradually, to the severe
for traitors, conspirators and witches.
[to skull] Do you doubt that there can be
such a thing as witchcraft?
You cannot deny the spirits.
Such assaults of Satan are certainly practised.
The weird sisters spoke falsely to Macbeth,
yet they were true.

Skull   How do you know that?

King   That much we learn from Scotland.
The Devil generally marks witches
With a private mark. He licks them
with his tongue in some privy part
before he receives them as his servants.

Skull   Filthy old lecher.

King   Therefore, witches have their hair
shaved off and their privates searched.
These witches went together by sea
in riddles and sieves
to the Kirk of North Berwick ...

Skull   Disgusting old paddlers.
What was wrong with their broomsticks?

King   Where, with flagons of wine
making merry with drink
they took hands on the land
and danced a reel singing

to the devil's trump.
And he was there in human form
and he commanded them to bend
and kiss his buttocks ...

Skull   Told you, didn't I?

King   ... as a sign of their devotion.
The witches asked the Devil ...

Skull   Before he hung his arse
over the pulpit, or after?

King   ... why he bore such hatred to the King?
And he said, 'Because the King
is the Devil's greatest enemy.'
And one of the witches took me aside
and told me the very words that passed
between the Queen and I in Norway
on the first night we were wed.

Skull   Is that all that passed then, Jamesie, words?

King   And when I was in Denmark
they took out a cat and christened it,
and tied it to the organs of a corpse
and cast it into the sea at Leith.

Skull   It's an old Scots tradition.

King   And our ship coming from Denmark
had a contrary wind
when all the rest sailed fair.

Skull   What happened to the geezer,
that had his arse
hanging over the pulpit?

King   He was taken and imprisoned
        and tried with the accustomed pain.
        First by throwing at his head with a rope.
        Second the nails on all his fingers
        were riven and pulled off
        with a pair of pincers.
        And under every nail
        was thrust in two needles
        up and over their heads.
        Thirdly, ...

Skull   There was more?

King   Lastly, he was put to the boots,
        The most severe and cruel pain.
        And after he received three strokes with the mallet
        he was asked if he would confess.

Skull   And?

King   But his tongue would not serve him
        to speak.

Skull   Would you believe it?

King   But the witches searched under his tongue
        and found two pins
        thrust up into his head.
        They showed how these charmed pins
        prevented him from confessing.

Skull   Now they tell us.

King   Then he was immediately released
        from the boots and brought to me
        and he confessed everything.

Skull   Bet you couldn't stop him.
        What happened to him in the end?

King   Burnt on the Castle Hill.
I just wish it could have been Bothwell,
but it was interesting all the same.

Skull   Scots theatre at its best.
Nothing to beat a good burning.

King   And justice was done.

Skull   Naturally.

King   I would not be cruel,
but they must obey.
The head must govern the body.

Skull   Or stay attached to it at least.

King   We use the gentler tortures first
proceeding gradually to the severe
for traitors, witches and conspirators.

Skull   Like Guy Fawkes, poor bloke.

King   I had to write permitting torture
by the English common law.
But then Guido confessed
the whole Popish plot
to blow me up with gunpowder.
He died for reasons of state.
I govern by my pen.

Skull   Oh yeh, sticks and stones will break my bones,
but words will never hurt me.
The prisoner will be drawn to his death
backwards at the horse's tail
because he has been retrograde to nature.
His head at ground denied the common air.
His privy parts will be cut off

and burnt before his face
since he was unworthily begotten
and unfit to leave generation after.
The bowels and heart will be hacked out.
The head that conceived the mischief
will be cut off. The trunk dismembered
to be publicly exposed.
That should just about do it.

King   A grateful people thanked God
for their Majestie's deliverance

Skull   Does that mean you're safe now, Daddy?

King   Of course, Charlie, we are all safe
As long as we obey God,
lawful rulers are defended by their subjects.

Skull   Will the bad Scots have their heads
cut off, Daddy, and be burnt?

King   All wrongdoers will undergo just punishment.

Skull   Are you God's right hand, Daddy?

King   Yes, Charles, as long as I obey Him
and rule as King

Skull   Am I special, too?

King   As long as you obey me, Charlie.

Skull   I'll always do everything you tell me.

King   Why, Charlie?

Skull   So as I keep my bleedin head.

King   No, no, laddie, your crown
So long as we keep our crowns.

Now settle down and go to sleep
We're going hunting in the morning.
[*puts skull down*]
Baloo, baloo, bairnie,
my bonnie wee Jamesie,
will your line stretch out to the crack of doom?
Aye, he points at them for mine.
[*Ghost is reappearing on other side*]
Oh no, not you again. Go away ...

Ghost   I am thy father's spirit
doomed for a certain time to walk the night
and for the day confined to fast in fires
till the foul crimes done in my days of nature
are burnt and purged away.

Skull   It's that Bucnahan, isn't it?

Ghost   List, list, o list,
if thou didst ever they dear father love.

Skull   Oh God.

Ghost   Revenge his foul and most unnatural murder.
But know thou, noble youth,
the serpent that did sting thy father's life
now wears his crown.

Skull   Bothwell!

King   Aye, Bothwell, that incestuous, that adulterate beast
with witchcraft of his wit, with traitorous gifts
won to his shameful lust
the will of his most seeming-virtuous queen.

Ghost   Oh what a falling off was there.
Adieu, adieu, remember me, remember me.

Skull   How could we forget you.
Are you alright, Jamesie?

King   And I was left alone, standing on the ramparts
gazing out across snow covered hills
shivering in the eerie light
the bitter cold north wind.
These are my father's lands, had he lived.
The very hills cry out for justice and revenge.
Buchanan hammers home their claim of right,
his detection of my mother.
I pray for Henry Darnley's soul,
the father that I never knew.

Skull   Papa, daddy.

King   Dead words to me.
Revenge, blood feud and counter feud
is all these children of Macbeth conceive.
The castle was awash with blood.
The drawn sword, the unsheathed dagger,
black deeds of violence through the generations.
Flesh torn and broken in the night.
Endings that vindicate new strife.
I am not a soldier or a fighter
but a King and poet. Beati pacifici.
Take away those weapons.
Give me back my books and pens.
Bring back the players. It's a lie.
I never banished them.
But I was afraid.
Among black-suited men with swords,
black-bearded men with Bibles.
Black-mantled women wearing out their knees

and crying for revenge.
Then he came to rescue me,
an eagle among crows.
Golden, fair and proud,
with Esmée I was happy
riding through wind and sun.
The clean sharp kill
followed by the glow of wine,
the music and the dancing,
skin to skin pressed close,
my self, possessing and receiving.
And in the Chapel Royal
heady incense of devotion.
sweet Jesu's alabaster body
adorned with wounds of kindness,
the Word made flesh,
warm loving flesh.

Skull	Corr! Corr!
King	Their wings are beating round my head.
	They're still watching me and waiting.
	My poor fool was left behind in Scotland.
Skull	Caw, caw.
Ghost	Come and sit you down. You shall not budge
	till I set you up a glass where you can see the inmost part.
	Be thou chaste as ice, as pure as snow,
	thou shalt not escape calumny.
	Or if thou needs marry, marry a fool;
	for wise men know well enough what monsters you make of them.

I have heard of your paintings too, well enough.
God hath given you one face and you make your-
selves another.
You jig, you amble, and you lisp and make your
wantonness your ignorance. Go, go to.

King   [*furtively takes mirror and make-up, proceeds to
make up in mime. He is upset now*]
Will you not come, Esmée
and visit my dreams?
Be my familiar one more time
before my eyes are closed forever.

Skull   My Lord, the actors are coming.

King   What an ass am I.
Aye, this is most brave.
That I, the son of the dear murdered,
prompted to my revenge, by heaven and hell
must like a whore unpack my heart with words
and fall a-cursing like a very drab.
I have heard that guilty creatures sitting at a play
have, by the very cunning of the scene,
been struck to the soul. That presently
they have proclaimed their malefactions.
For murder though it have no tongue will speak
I'll have a play something like
the murder of my father.
You're welcome, masters, welcome all.
Speak the speech, I pray you as I pronounce it to
you – trippingly on the tongue. Don't saw the air
too much with your hand, thus, but use all gently.

Decorum is the soul of rhetoric. Let your own discretion be your dominie. Suit the action to the word, the word to the action, with this special observance: that you o'erstep not the modesty of nature. For anything so overdone is from the purpose of playing, whose end, both at the first and now, was and is to hold as 'twere the mirror up to nature

Skull   You don't half look an idiot.

King   And let those that play your clowns speak no more than is set down for them; for there be of them that will themselves laugh to set on some quantity of barren spectators to laugh too, though in the meantime some necessary question of the play be then considered. That's villainous and shows a most pitiful ambition in the fool that uses it. Go make you ready.

[*King and skull take up position as spectators*]

King   [*beginning in a neutral tone*]
Enter a king and queen very lovingly, the queen embracing him. He is weak and leans on her. She kneels and protests her love. He sits upon a bed and takes her up beside him, his head upon her neck and breasts. She lays him down on his sickbed and holds a healing cup for him to drink. He sinks back on the pillows. She watches and, seeing him asleep, withdraws.
In another part, two black-hooded men approach carrying a barrel. They set it down and move away. A bang is heard. [*He provides a bang.*] The king falls from his bed and crawls along the floor. One of the hooded men returns. He kneels beside the king.

He puts his cloak over the king's mouth. He presses hard and presses. He wriggles, he presses ...
In another place the queen appears. She weeps and cries for help. A black-cloaked man enters...

Skull   Bothwell.

King   ... and takes her in his arms, but other black hooded figures enter. They seize the queen and drag her away.

[*The King has to speak quickly now.*]

In another place, the queen appears between two black-hooded men. One holds an axe. Taking off her cloak, the queen bares her neck and bends her head. The axe is raised above her and brought down.
[*A second bang. The King is in severe distress*]
Her bloody head appears
dancing in the air.

Skull   Help, help the king!

King   Sweet Jesus, help me.
I was cast upon thee from the womb.
Thou are my God from my mother's belly.
Be not far from me for trouble is near.
My God, my God.

[*sobbing*]

I was alone without father or mother,
brother or sister.
King of Scots and heir to the realm of England.
God save the King. [*Looks to skull*]

Skull   God save the King!

[*King bringing himself under control.*]

King   Please be composed, friends.
O'erstep not the modesty of nature.
It is true, the Queen our mother has died.
We have dispatches from England.

Skull   Let the dispatches be read aloud.
When the Queen was seated in the fatal chair she
heard the death warrants read by the clerk ...

King   ... with an appearance of indifference. Nor did she
seem more attentive to the devotional exercises in
which, as a Catholic, she could not conscientiously
join. She implored the mercy of heaven, after the
form proscribed by her own Church. She then
prepared herself for execution, taking off such parts
of her dress as might interfere with the deadly blow.
The executioners offered their assistance, but she
modestly refused it, saying she had neither been
accustomed to undress before so many spectators
nor to be served by such grooms of the chamber.
She quietly chid her maids, who were unable to
withhold their cries of lamentation and reminded
them that she had engaged for their silence. Last of
all, she laid her head on the block, which the
executioners severed from her body with two strokes
of the axe. The headsman held it up in his hand,
and the Dean cried out, 'So perish all Queen
Elizabeth's enemies!' No voice, save that of the Earl
of Kent, could answer Amen: the rest were choked
with sobs and tears.

[*A very awkward pause as he struggles for control –
indication of stammer*]

King   We shall write to our royal cousin, Elizabeth
to enquire more closely into these grave matters.
Tis true I am a cradle King
yet do remember every thing
that I have heretofore put out
and yet begin not for to doubt.

Ghost   [*whispered*] She was a whure, Jamesie, and a
murderess
She deserved it.
A snake that deserved to die.

Skull   Nothing was proved against her.
It was all them, forgeries and lies.
Could you not have done something, Jamesie,
to help her?

Ghost   Bothwell tried to help her.

Skull   And look where he ended up.

King   A marble catafalque shall be raised
to my late mother's memory.
In Westminster Abbey.
I shall ascertain how and why she died.

Ghost   She had her heid cut aff.
Hacked clean like Guido Fawkes.
You remember him.
He nearly blew you to smithereens
like your faither.

Skull   He never knew him.

King   [*sings*] Allie, ballie, ballie, ballie, bee
Sittin on your mammie's knee
Greeting for a wee bawbee

	Tae buy some succour ... candy. That's why I love you so much, Charlie. Why I need you to love me even more.

Ghost   Aye, Charlie's his mammy's boy.

King   I should never have left Scotland.

Skull   Better the devil you know.

King   And now my poor fool is hanged.

Skull   No, no life? Why should a dog,
         a horse, a rat, have life?

King   And you no breath at all.

[*The skull is now dead*]

Where are your gibes and gambols now? Quite
chop-fallen. Now get you to my lady's chamber and
tell her let her paint an inch thick to this favour she
must come. Make her laugh at that.
[*The King raises the skull in the air*]
Hail, King, for so thou art,
behold where stands
the usurper's cursed head.
Hail, King of Scotland.
[*The King puts the skull in its final position*]
Uneasy lies the head.
[*The King stands to pray*]
Thou art he that tookest me out of the womb.
Thou madest me to hope when I was on my
mother's breasts
I was cast upon thee from the womb.
Thou art my God from my mother's belly.
Be not far from me for trouble is near. Amen.

[*The King takes off his robe and bundles it up in his arms like a baby*]

The little drooping mouth and the cheek
ruffed up. My love,
where are you walking and with whom for a friend?
Just on the verge.

[*The King lays the baby in his chair*]

Look, look on the lips.

[*to audience*]

Tell the bairn a tale tae soothe an solace him.
Aye, once upon a time there was a king.

[*leaving*]

Don't disturb my peace.
Alone at last. [*Exits*]

Airthra

Airthra

One

Fire in the agate
bubbling lava veining quartz
mica flaking
Schist Uchil hard watcher of the folding sandstone
settled layers ice sculpted
sedimenting water soils seeding trees and ferns
bog mosses, rushes, the river slowly flows through.

Two

Beite	Birch	
Hazel	Codd	
Oak	Dur	GUARD
Aspen	Eagh	
Fearn	Alder	STREAM
Gath	Ivy	
Huath	Whitebeam	
Iogh	Yew	SHADING
Rowan	Luis	
Nuin	Ash	BRAE
Peith	Pine	
Ruse	Elder	
Suie	Willow	CLEFT
Teine	Furze	
Ur	Heather	MUIR

Three

Seven swans
white necks outstretched
geese thirteen sounding southwards from the ice
two herons poise stilted on the firth.
One hovering kestrel
and the long upwind water winds gently
to the hard blue salt chopping race
north crested Sea

Eye sweeps Eagle cruises
Uchil Range Campsie Fells
Barrier of Bannog
to the distant sun-reflecting bens.
Scatter of deer on Drumnach ridge
rising from the marsh,
wood-spread shelters squirrel and fox,
beaver otter badger bear.

Wolves stake north
running reindeer red pull down
the wild white bull winter-weakened
wary of the seven pointer Stag
belling in the spring.

Four

Two hundred years on open plains
I lived a herd in shape of ox.

Three hundred years of covered canopy
wild boar of trees tusk master.

Five hundred years was still
an ancient form of bird
on heron's wings.

One thousand mottled years
a silver salmon in the flood.

A fisher caught me in his net
The woman dressed me lovingly
She ate alone, her belly swelled
And I slipped out a twisting snake.

Issue of woman I was born
One hundred years
a bloomin man.

Five

Climbing upwards
zig-zag through the oaks
birch rowan furze and ash
fringe the burn's deep channel
cutting to the ridge.

Against the sky gawky fast
gold clasped on white memoriser of the tribe
gateway to rebirth in training
hard druid discipline, absent youth.

Long legs stretch out towards the Dun.
Shifting on the slope brown movement
turns the eye. Girl not deer. Watches.
She climbs steady to the brow.

He follows crossways to intersect
her path but crouches low.
Hair tied back heading for the pool
to bathe in springtime
no splashing children but alone.

Turn back or track every coiling step.
Silent in the heather gently fingers yellow broom
to see the low set water rushes edging rippled surface
in the cold clear blue and white hill air
lifting from the foot the skin rolls up
thigh hair brown belly shoulder white
against the golden neck.

She wades into the pool
rushes part arms screened across her breasts.
One swift opening aureoles to the sun
elbows wide like wings she drops on the surface wake
the neck a prow pent up breath releasing,
he turns quickly back still unnoticed
homes to his mother's hearth.

Six

The black month comes
ice thickens
lamps burn in shelters
sickness hunger,
death moves free.

Sometimes the sky
is hung with lights
above the mountain,
waits the narrow day.

First the preparation.
Water poured in stone
pure cold.

Second gathering
embers from each hearth
borne to the circle.

Third the tryst
of fire and water
sun and rain
in hissing union.

Fourth the washing
water carried to each house
garments stripped
lustration.

Vigil fifth
a round of dark and light
we fast inside
the chamber of the dead.

That night the Sun
confirms
one lingering setting
down the passage.

Night
Long
Dread

Fire signals
torches flicker
light and water
laid on stone
a silver gleam

Sunrise through the pillars
two mounds of stone
warmed by life
the golden throat will sound again.

Seven

I got up early and slipped away without breakfast.
Over the estate wall and up the tussocky field rabbits bobbing.
The dyke tumbled long ago topped now with stob and wire,
I once saw roebuck clear it in a single grace-powered bound.
Between the wires I go and in among a fringe of trees,
windbreak and storm shelter for the spread of loch and park.
I come out into light, rinsed in dew,
water in the shadow of the wooded hill,
trees dawn-leaved with mist.
I cut round the western end, rhododendrons shouting for the sun.
Double Dykes, Roman Cutting, Parkhead,
Highlandman's Well, the Devil's Turn to Logie.

I turn east instead along the shaded shore,
short cut on a summer morning, suddenly taut,
tugged by an absence, I start towards the Stone,
upright on the gentle brow twice my height untoppled.
Now I hear feet pound on the ground
racing past the green, down the track.
Across barbed wire islanded with stalks of barley
one last burst the sandstone sentinel is in my arms
pressed sunwarm palms caress the weathered face
but cannot meet rough join sob-tearing now this other touch.

Without you husked chaff called out before I knew
myself this morning chased for life.

Eight

He travels the drovers' way by Blackford and Dunblane
up onto the muir and down again at Logie.
Clouds becalm windless air
feet sore and itchy whirr of flies, bees buzz
grass dried thistledown drifting .
The staff slows its strike at Highlandman's well
a trickle barely dampens tongue and lips.
The last twisting drop to Logie by the Devil's Turn.
Through leafy shade the cleft smooths out
green pasture by a bubbling burn
a welcome hut in sheltered grove.
Touch of water tingling on the feet
a hirpling canopy of light and shade
no flash of swift or swallow, the lull a humming solitude
the saintly Serf slips into sleep.

Green island off the shore sea birds solitary call
the white foam breaks on sandy beach
upborne a floating coracle in silver stream of fish
a maiden's naked form
alabaster numb chastened by the sea.
Lift her gently in the sealskin
broken on a chariot's axle thrown down the rock face
a king set fast against her vows
rapes her dream of holiness
a baby in her womb complete and fragile
cast adrift into the estuary the sacred cargo comes
guided by the waves around a blessed circling isle.
Lower her softly by the ashes
healing warmth gives life and movement to the limbs

while in the watery globe a pulse begins to beat
stirring for the gates of birth
tugged and pulled towards the light.

Dreaming Kentigern
here in the druid grove
Saint Serf will plant his Shepherd's crook

Nine

Early morning on the hill climbing past Parkhead
a surge of sheep burst over Fossachie
break on the rocky crest a wash of grey on green
bleating wildly bunching gaggle-bound to a reluctant front.
Till over come the dogs racing round untidy edges
whistling sweep of stragglers in the bobbing flotsam.
I swing the outer gate and let the tide flow in.
The shepherd follows last and pulls the gate behind
crook on arm content to see them fanked
heaving backs and rumps cool
standing time for thick strong tea and smoke.
I set up the platform winding cable round the pole
unroll woolsacks stacking blades in boxes
prising cans of buist and scrape irons clean.
Jera, Drumbrae, Pendreich and Fossachie himself they come
quiet men before a long day's shearing
The sun warms to its task
but before the buzzing scrape of shears
I listen to the rising dew
broken only by the baa of the lambs and breath of black-nosed
    yows,
brown eyes wait to be shorn quivering to break loose
sprung free of winter's weight a pure white stream in spate
migrating to the mountain pasture
till driven down in autumn speaned and culled
to face another winter.

Ten

Deid wasted dwined awa fower or five months syne
aw bane an skin an een.
He pit up his hay an drave his kye tae pasture
though aye wi a buik tae haun.
Buiks mair buiks an music is aw he has tae wull.
There wis nae hairm in the puir body
gentle born he wis, a courtier an notary
gied awthing fur Christ
fur he hasna muckle gear.
He raisit a bonnie psaulm o Sundays
an whan he climbit tae the desk he kent a siccar wurd
nae papist clishmaclavers
dreamin een forbye an aye a winsome sough o grace.
Noo he's traivellin tae his ain kirkyaird.
Frae aw the airts they come
meenisters o Stirling, Kippen an Dunblane an furth o Edinburgh
black-coatit gentry wi Bibles tae their oxters.
The Lairds arrive as weill, chappin tane aifter tither at the door
Menstrie, Gogar, Corntoun, Powis, Airthrey passit ben.
The coffin's cairrit oot a feck o fowk staunin roond
women wan wi greetin.
The meenisters gang foremaist,
the Lairds theirsels tak up the box, respectin their ain kind.
Awthing quaet forbye the cheepin o the birds.
Airthrey gies the wurd.
Shoon thud in step, herts stound sobs sneckit
the men cam in ahent a lang daurk snake creepin tae the kirk.
The bell begoud tae toll
ye gates lift up your heids – nae settled custom noo –
wurds risin oan the sough fa back

till ane sair body pits up a line
an ithers gie it back,
here an there then aw aroond
a single swell o voice.
Lord from the depths
to thee I cry
gie an attentive ear
mair than the morning watch
my saul bides for the Lord.
Ilk ane taks his cord
broon yird heapit oan green grass
wurds lowerin in the grave, stanes rattle gin the wud
folk shiftit turn awa, kent haunds grippit.
He wis a guid man the meenister
noo he's in the grund,
I maun awa tae the sowin.

Eleven

On an afternoon of slate grey skies, cracked ice underfoot
I took the sheltered back road
Hermitage Wood to Logie.
Flurries of snow-packed clouds
refused to give the comfort of a fall,
bone trees ribbed above the track
tensed northwards on the slope.

What kind of hermit lived up there,
a cell beneath the cliff and steps cut into the rock?
He could survey the Forth
or walk along the Carlie Craig where high above the kirk
women by ordeal were cast down to the Devil.
More like a Laird's notion,
hermit wanted for a final touch
to his wild ordered fashion.
He stepped back to admire and tumbled down the steps.
Tales of an unlucky breed, young heirs repeatedly drown
dropping through black icy holes that shiver on old fault lines.

Swing on halfway to Logie when freeze stock still
the seven-pointer guards the crossroads
head erect, nose twitching at the scent,
his chest held high on stilts,
the winter king in exile.

Liquid eyes long gaze of time
he turns canters off into the wood
through which he came foraging into the yards.
I follow his old memory into the ruins of a farm
eyeless cottages where children played
cobbled barns and tumbled byres.
Their people died in some great freeze
migrated to a warmer land or drifted
leaving mouldered ruins to remember.

The stag and I stand witness.
They walked like me to Logie where crowstepped gable
surmounted by an empty belfry through which the snow squalls
stands sentinel on tumbling seas of stone,
scythes and skulls, the mason's square
an hour glass and winged angels.
Voices blown round roofless walls
or the wind's own sterile breath.

Twelve

Tak me tae him, Ellen

No again, Lassie

Aye but he was bonny buirdly till they cut him doon
wi the plaidie wrappit roon him lik a gowan tree in flooer
ainly aw the flooers waur reid.

Ah ken, Lassie

He wis a strang aik till they stickit him wi cauld airn.
Cam tae the windae, Ellen, he's taen awa
jist an auld stump bidin.

Yer faither struck it doon years syne
Dae ye no mind oan yer faither?

I mind the meenister, the daurk-coatit hoodie,
wham I cryit faither. Peck, peck peckin. He
pit me tae the stool an shamit me.
Pyke oot yer bonnie blue een
but I hae ma gounie an I wis jauntie
whan the Prince dauncit at Halyrude.
The King's gane ower the water, Ellen,
but dinnay clype, dinna speir. Davie's wi him.

Aiblins he is, Lassie, aiblins he's gane tae France.

Dinna lee tae me. Davie's deid an kisted in Logie kirkyaird.
The meenister pit him there an draggit doon the tree
that I micht see him moulder.
Thaur's yer filthy Jacobite – tak yer fill o his stinkin flesh.

Wheesht noo, Lassie, an we'll gang
tae the grave an set flooers at his stane.

I'll no gang but I kin dress in ma gounie.
Shaw yer braw duds, lass an we'll mak a florish fur douce
    Edinbro.
Rags an tatters lik petals o flooers tae cast oan the grund.
They'll no kin howk him oot, no cairt the corp awa.
He disna belang tae her reid-heidit whure.
I'm come tae tak ma man hame. Hielan bitch,
I'll stick ye wi cauld airn lik ma faither telt me.

Shoosh, Lassie, shoosh, we'll gang tae his grave.

Aye it's ma ainly launmerk noo, the kirkyaird stane.

Dinna tak oan sae sair, Lassie, they're aw gane lang syne
an I pledgit tae yer mither ah wud mind ye,
we'll mak a fine florish steppin oot frae Blalowan
wi cockades tae oor bonnets an nae meenister tae thwart us.

I'm cauld, Ellen, cauld tae the marrow.
Bide a wee an pit ma heid tae yer breist.
Haud me ticht in yer airms an sing a sang tae mak the waesome
    hert licht.

The wind doth blaw today ma luve
an a few sma drops o rain
I never had but ain true luve
in cauld grave he is lain
in cauld grave he is lain

Thirteen

Light spills out through open doors onto the early summer dark
flame flickering in the mantles draws up the gallery stairs
lookout over decks of pews packed for the Communion Season.
Mass of bodies and above the play of glow and shadow waves
    on timber beams of sound ascending to the loft.
Come unto me the preacher says
all you that labour and are heavy laden
and I will give you rest.
Assembling voices filter through
Beloved in the Lord attend

Lippen tae the wurd

I have received of the Lord
the same night in which he was
betrayed Lord Jesus Christ
took bread

Through your goodness
we have this bread to offer
which earth has given
and human hands have made
It will become for us
the bread of life

Blissit be God for all his giftis

After the same manner also
He took the cup saying
this cup is the new testament
in my blood this do
as oft as ye drink of it

in remembrance of me

Through your goodness
we have this wine to offer
fruit of the vine
and work of human hands
it will become our spiritual drink

Blissit be God for all his giftis

Ye do shew forth
the Lord's death
till He comes

Lord we are not worthy
Lord we are not worthy
Cast yourselves not down to the daurk within
Lift up your eyes to see the Saviour's gracious light
Up to the throne of grace dear one draw near
lay down your burden at the mercy seat
Lippen tae ane tender wurd
sweet awe and trembling yokit gently by the Son o God

Sanctus Sanctus Sanctus
Dominus Deus Sabaoth
sanctus sanctus sanctus
pleni sunt coeli et terra
gloriae tuae
Hosanna in excelsis

not as we ought
but as we are able

Lord hae mercie
Christ hae mercie

Agnus Dei
qui tollit peccata mundi
grant us your peace

Bodie o Christ
Body of Christ
Blude o Christ
Blood of Christ

rising to the flow raftered glory
weightless free wingless white

Fourteen

On Drumbrae stand
a hemisphere of stars above
the carse outspread below
a patchwork of black fields
and blinking lights down river.
warm darkness of summer fields ingathered
the folded scent of flowers
sap enclosed burst out
across the sky
a million seeds of fire.

Stirling Brig a stand
the Forth flows gently through
the arches of a midnight crossing
wash white dissolving down
a staring disc of moonshine
intent upon a silver stream
of fingers playing
now particle now wave upon the water
yours is the cool compelling
moon music dancing

On the move between
along the Causeway striding out
thighs and stomach chest and arms
mind lull takes control
stretching legs to woo
a landscape that changed shape
two fixed points merge
selves unselve
flesh and spirit tryst
at Logie

Fifteen

Wheel high on curve of cloud and sun
airborne in the current flow to the mountain
across a dappled loch
through groves of trees soft turning on the wind
oak elm ash
and sheen of silver birch leaves
nod delicately between the rocks
rivulets of deer step to the hill in coats of autumn red
heads held high bear time's insignia.
People raise their narrow beds
toppling death's dark scythemen
stones crack apart
grains run from the hourglass to join the washing stream
mould and lichen memory leave
in body of light earth rises to greet the revenants
I not-I, you not-you in death
in life forever Airthra

Some other books published by **LUATH** PRESS

POETRY

Drink the Green Fairy
Brian Whittingham
ISBN 1 84282 020 6 PB £8.99

Tartan & Turban
Bashabi Fraser
ISBN 1 84282 044 3 PB £8.99

The Ruba'iyat of Omar Khayyam, in Scots
Rab Wilson
ISBN 1 84282 046 X PB £8.99

Talking with Tongues
Brian D. Finch
ISBN 1 84282 006 0 PB £8.99

Kate o Shanter's Tale and other poems [book]
Matthew Fitt
ISBN 1 84282 028 1 PB £6.99

Kate o Shanter's Tale and other poems [audio CD]
Matthew Fitt
ISBN 1 84282 043 5 PB £9.99

Bad Ass Raindrop
Kokumo Rocks
ISBN 1 84282 018 4 PB £6.99

Madame Fifi's Farewell and other poems
Gerry Cambridge
ISBN 1 84282 005 2 PB £8.99

Poems to be Read Aloud
introduced by Tom Atkinson
ISBN 0 946487 00 6 PB £5.00

Scots Poems to be Read Aloud
introduced by Stuart McHardy
ISBN 0 946487 81 2 PB £5.00

Picking Brambles
Des Dillon
ISBN 1 84282 021 4 PB £6.99

Sex, Death & Football
Alistair Findlay
ISBN 1 84282 022 2 PB £6.99

The Luath Burns Companion
John Cairney
ISBN 1 84282 000 1 PB £10.00

Immortal Memories: A Compilation of Toasts to the Memory of Burns as delivered at Burns Suppers, 1801-2001
John Cairney
ISBN 1 84282 009 5 HB £20.00

The Whisky Muse: Scotch whisky in poem & song
Robin Laing
ISBN 1 84282 041 9 PB £7.99

FICTION

Torch
Lin Anderson
ISBN 1 84282 042 7 PB £9.99

Heartland
John MacKay
ISBN 1 84282 059 1 PB £9.99

The Blue Moon Book
Anne MacLeod
ISBN 1 84282 061 3 PB £9.99

The Glasgow Dragon
Des Dillon
ISBN 1 84282 056 7 PB £9.99

Driftnet
Lin Anderson
ISBN 1 84282 034 6 PB £9.99

The Fundamentals of New Caledonia
David Nicol
ISBN 1 84282 93 6 HB £16.99

Milk Treading
Nick Smith
ISBN 1 84282 037 0 PB £6.99

The Road Dance
John MacKay
ISBN 1 84282 024 9 PB £6.99

The Strange Case of RL Stevenson
Richard Woodhead
ISBN 0 946487 86 3 HB £16.99

But n Ben A-Go-Go
Matthew Fitt
ISBN 0 946487 82 0 HB £10.99
ISBN 1 84282 014 1 PB £6.99

The Bannockburn Years
William Scott
ISBN 0 946487 34 0 PB £7.95

Outlandish Affairs: An Anthology of Amorous Encounters
Edited and introduced by Evan Rosenthal and Amanda Robinson
ISBN 1 84282 055 9 PB £9.99

FOLKLORE

Scotland: Myth Legend & Folklore
Stuart McHardy
ISBN 0 946487 69 3 PB £7.99

The Supernatural Highlands
Francis Thompson
ISBN 0 946487 31 6 PB £8.99

Tall Tales from an Island
Peter Macnab
ISBN 0 946487 07 3 PB £8.99

Tales from the North Coast
Alan Temperley
ISBN 0 946487 18 9 PB £8.99

THE QUEST FOR

The Quest for Robert Louis Stevenson
John Cairney
ISBN 0 946487 87 1 HB £16.99

The Quest for the Nine Maidens
Stuart McHardy
ISBN 0 946487 66 9 HB £16.99

The Quest for the Original Horse Whisperers
Russell Lyon
ISBN 1 842820 020 6 HB £16.99

The Quest for the Celtic Key
Karen Ralls-MacLeod and
Ian Robertson
ISBN 1 842820 031 1 PB £8.99

The Quest for Arthur
Stuart McHardy
ISBN 1 842820 12 5 HB £16.99

The Quest for Charles Rennie Mackintosh
John Cairney
ISBN 1 84282 058 3 HB £16.99

ON THE TRAIL OF

On the Trail of John Muir
Cherry Good
ISBN 0 946487 62 6 PB £7.99

On the Trail of Mary Queen of Scots
J. Keith Cheetham
ISBN 0 946487 50 2 PB £7.99

On the Trail of William Wallace
David R. Ross
ISBN 0 946487 47 2 PB £7.99

On the Trail of Robert Burns
John Cairney
ISBN 0 946487 51 0 PB £7.99

On the Trail of Bonnie Prince Charlie
David R. Ross
ISBN 0 946487 68 5 PB £7.99

On the Trail of Queen Victoria in the Highlands
Ian R. Mitchell
ISBN 0 946487 79 0 PB £7.99

On the Trail of Robert the Bruce
David R. Ross
ISBN 0 946487 52 9 PB £7.99

On the Trail of Robert Service
GW Lockhart
ISBN 0 946487 24 3 PB £7.99

LANGUAGE

Luath Scots Language Learner [Book]
L Colin Wilson
ISBN 0 946487 91 X PB £9.99

Luath Scots Language Learner [Double Audio CD Set]
L Colin Wilson
ISBN 1 84282 026 5 CD £16.99

WALK WITH LUATH

Mountain Days & Bothy Nights
Dave Brown and Ian Mitchell
ISBN 0 946487 15 4 PB £7.50

The Joy of Hillwalking
Ralph Storer
ISBN 1 84282 069 9 PB £7.50

Scotland's Mountains before the Mountaineers
Ian R. Mitchell
ISBN 0 946487 39 1 PB £9.99

Mountain Outlaw
Ian R. Mitchell
ISBN 1 84282 027 3 PB £6.50

NEW SCOTLAND

Some Assembly Required: behind the scenes at the rebirth of the Scottish Parliament
Andy Wightman
ISBN 0 946487 84 7 PB £7.99

Scotland - Land and Power the agenda for land reform
Andy Wightman
ISBN 0 946487 70 7 PB £5.00

Old Scotland New Scotland
Jeff Fallow
ISBN 0 946487 40 5 PB £6.99

Notes from the North Incorporating a Brief History of the Scots and the English
Emma Wood
ISBN 0 946487 46 4 PB £8.99

Scotlands of the Future: sustainability in a small nation
Edited by Eurig Scandrett
ISBN 1 84282 035 4 PB £7.99

Eurovision or American Dream? Britain, the Euro and the future of Europe
David Purdy
ISBN 1 84282 036 2 PB £3.99

HISTORY

Reportage Scotland: History in the Making
Louise Yeoman
ISBN 1 84282 051 6 PB £6.99

A Passion for Scotland
David R. Ross
ISBN 1 84282 019 2 PB £5.99

Scots in Canada
Jenni Calder
ISBN 1 84282 038 9 PB £7.99

Plaids & Bandanas: Highland Drover to Wild West Cowboy
Rob Gibson
ISBN 0 946487 88 X PB £7.99

Luath Press Limited

committed to publishing well written books worth reading

LUATH PRESS takes its name from Robert Burns, whose little collie Luath (*Gael.*, swift or nimble) tripped up Jean Armour at a wedding and gave him the chance to speak to the woman who was to be his wife and the abiding love of his life. Burns called one of *The Twa Dogs* Luath after Cuchullin's hunting dog in *Ossian's Fingal*. Luath Press was established in 1981 in the heart of Burns country, and is now based a few steps up the road from Burns' first lodgings on Edinburgh's Royal Mile.

Luath offers you distinctive writing with a hint of unexpected pleasures.

Most bookshops in the UK, the US, Canada, Australia, New Zealand and parts of Europe either carry our books in stock or can order them for you. To order direct from us, please send a £sterling cheque, postal order, international money order or your credit card details (number, address of cardholder and expiry date) to us at the address below. Please add post and packing as follows: UK – £1.00 per delivery address; overseas surface mail – £2.50 per delivery address; overseas airmail – £3.50 for the first book to each delivery address, plus £1.00 for each additional book by airmail to the same address. If your order is a gift, we will happily enclose your card or message at no extra charge.

Luath Press Limited
543/2 Castlehill
The Royal Mile
Edinburgh EH1 2ND
Scotland
Telephone: 0131 225 4326 (24 hours)
Fax: 0131 225 4324
email: gavin.macdougall@luath.co.uk
Website: www.luath.co.uk